T0162110

PRAEDER'S LETTERS

ALSO BY JAMES BAKER HALL

Poetry

Fiction

Photography

PRAEDER'S LETTERS

Sarabande Books
LOUISVILLE, KENTUCKY

No part of this book may be reproduced without written permission of the publisher. Please direct inquiries to:

Managing Editor
Sarabande Books, Inc.
2234 Dundee Road, Suite 200
Louisville, KY 40205

LIBRARY OF CONGRESS CATALOGING-IN-PUBLICATION DATA

Hall, James Baker, 1935–
    Praeder's letters / by James Baker Hall. — 1st ed.
        p.   cm.
    ISBN 1-889330-80-9 (cloth : acid-free paper) —
ISBN 1-889330-79-5 (pbk. : acid-free paper)
I. Title.
PS3558.A3685 P74 2002
811'.54—dc21   2002001260

Cover photograph of Barry Spacks by James Baker Hall.

Cover and text design by Charles Casey Martin.

A portion of this book appeared, in a different form, in *The Paris Review* #87.

Manufactured in the United States of America.
This book is printed on acid-free paper.

Sarabande Books is a nonprofit literary organization.

Funded in part by a grant from the Kentucky Arts Council, a state agency of the Education, Arts, and Humanities Cabinet.

FIRST EDITION

ONE

1.15.1956/sjpr / Dear Billy my lad

Through channels as intricate as life
itself I have at hand a copy of Stylus
Thank you thank you   Indeed

I am not dead though more
I cannot say

                You are God
bless you one of the three
people in the world who
conceivably could care

I sound intolerably grim
about it after all
it is a witty poem worthy
of your fine mind
                & I am honored
to find my name attached honored
is hardly the word

                but frankly
excuse me I am moved by this
deeply &
as usual
unable to express
myself forgive
me

            Thank you thank you but Billy
it does take me back your poem
hurls me back
with such emptiness

to our cold days in Lex the Toddle House
the Green Dome & Fetterman with his stinking
dogs
      Tell me how I fell into the house
of a weightlifter will you
                & Winston
with his ascots & chemistry set
The man actually slept in my bed
his beard each morning stuck up
into the fetid air
         & Grant C
keeping his profile among the press
of students   I miss
the man
      But I have forgotten
the name of the lady in your peom
poem excuse me
          though I do recall
her suave tongue & vaginal intensity

& her squalid mind
which I now forgive

         Poetry indeed
redeems you are far the better poet
Billy I could not have written
such incisive lines for that dark lady
I being the blackest spot in the pot
Thank you/

      If the day
were longer my memory
better I would try
to account for myself

                               James Baker Hall

since I left Lexington your town
of sweetness & light but
it is no story anyway
what the hell

        I never
had business in a university
not for a minute as I am sure
you well know

        I was
in NYC for a while worked
as a bellhop fill in
the blanks

        Am now
in the Coast Guard
again & at my own request
in San Juan where
at the moment I sit
with newly bought pad & pen
in a cafe

        They speak Spanish
here which is fine with me
shake hands over my head
which isn't

        I am not Gauguin
nor as the saying goes
was meant to be

        but it is true
Billy that I have bought this pad

& pen on the strength
of your peom
              there I go again
poem   Get a hold of yourself
Praeder

              On *your*
strength it is   These
are the first words
I have written in who knows
& who cares

              SJ
is no Hawaii thank God
Latins seem to be in my fate
& there are certainly worse people
in the world

              Dignity
is upheld here
by pissing in the streets
Their honor is agreeable
to me
              even if they do
shake hands over my head

& what more can one ask
in this life

              I quit
this else I begin to sound
like Ernest Hemingway
your affection for the man
notwithstanding   How Ezra

James Baker Hall

tolerated such a child even
for the purpose of teaching him
is beyond me
but then Ezra
usually is

      The truth is
& it always comes out always
I had in mind with the purchase
of this pad & pen not simply
to thank you for your elegant
& generous dedication but to make
of the same stroke an effort
of my own

      A Dimensions #3
sort of thing cafe
hand wrestling in the colors
of Jacob with the angel faint
afterimage
         if I do not enlarge
myself insufferably
         of the spirit
of the dead watching no caps
you know the kind

        and offer
it to your fine magazine
More of that later if more
indeed there is   ///

I am a radio operator
I work 32 hours a week

I have enough money
I drink some
I fuck some
I read some
mostly history
I stalk barracuda
the only danger
I enjoy

Well
that is done with
& it didn't take long
What now

I am as shy
as a young thing my hands
go to pieces

Your poem
Praeder you even spelled it
right now
to it

Is this
any way to write
an old friend
Is this any way
to do anything

Imagine here three asterisks
& an ampersand signifying
a lifetime spent between
that last sentence
& this

James Baker Hall

In which of course
I completed a serious study
of Ezra
            Have you read
Section: Rock Drill
It is no Pisan Cantos
but then what is

                    & even wrote
my dissertation   The total light
process a single Chinese character
scratched with a hunting knife
on the side of my zippo lighter

Tell them about me
at Harvard I'm sure
you will

It isn't Latins in my fate
it's the sea

                    I will probably end
up mesmerized by agony staring
into the eye of a flying fish
Then the long last header
into the brine

                    If I can ever
overcome my embarrassment //

* * *

Dear Billy   It is late
at night there are rats

under my bed within the hour
the whine of garbage trucks
in Calle Sol
         & there is no
poem   There is no
poem

     Van Gogh wanted to kill
Gauguin with a razor but cut
himself instead
             & sent
the issue to a whore
It loves to happen
Before sleep that night
swaddled in the bandages
of his next self-portrait
he placed a lighted candle
in the window in hope
that she would come

Can you believe it
I can

    Enough
enough I send a verse
instead   Beware of men
who use meter & rhyme
& other men's matter

        Dimensions #3
      (for Odysseus Adams me not dead)

There was this woman
Who lived in an ether of sighs

                                        James Baker Hall

The devil lived in her finger
And Kinsey looked out of her eyes

Enough indeed   Write me
if this does not depress
you beyond repair

Love & kisses Paul

* * *

& who pray is this Baxter Adams
Have you finally become
the Maxwell Street Presbyterian Church
Got vocabulary cards in pocket
Wm. Baxter Adams would be bad enough
You are as insufferable as I am
& who would have thought it
Face it Billy
you are just Billy
even to those who love you best
Tell your grandmother I said hi
& be sure to collect your paper route
before the 10th of the month

The only hope for a poet
is to learn first to pick
his nose you know that
if you don't just ask

Paul

1.30.56/SJPR
Dear Billy & Billirenes

Why of course I know Kathleen
& a pox on her for not remembering
I knew I was never in Lexington not
for a minute
                    Remind her Billy
Baxter Adams if you please of that grim
blackguard who came to see her
in the hospital with Bracket

Now do you remember
                    I said
not a word hung at the door
one foot on top the other
like a minor Dickens come
upon a sweet shop window

& said not a word

Pray what could I say
in the presence of such
beauty such suffering
She had misused her arm
on a motorcyle if I am not
mistaken
                    which impressed me
mightily
                    though I would never
for one minute have admitted it
never

        Her brother was there

James Baker Hall

or if he wasn't I imagined him
& in addition to my general
embarrassment my silence
was due to no uncertain dislike
of the man

      He was not only
better educated & better looking
than I
      but more intimate
with the young lady

for which I will never
forgive him /

      All these warts
& elbows confuse & irritate you
I am sure as well they should
you forgetful hussy

But the awful truth is I am
at deep heart a rather simple
& sentimental fool
        & I
had rather confuse & irritate
than embarrass

      To embarrass
is the only unforgiveable sin

I am sure you have had your fill
of congratulations & felicitations
so congratulations & felicitations/
There is only one thing I have

ever
wanted in this miserable life
from time to time I see it clearly
& even though infrequently admit
it to myself & that
hold on to your seats
is a wife

sovegna vos

      Poetry
is the sole tolerable occupation
only because love is so
difficult   I was going
to say impossible

but given the occasion
that would be
in bad taste

      Please
pay no attention to me
life is difficult enough
as it is

      Not even a wife
I often suspect since I am
sure the dignities of marriage
are beyond me
          leave love out
of it you will have to sooner
or later anyway

but a mother

James Baker Hall

for my children
That this will never
come to pass is one
of the few recommendations
left for the world

          Enough
of this I had in mind ceremony
as I always do & lest you think
I am a fraud here my children
of sweetness & light is what
I propose to wit

          // BUT FIRST
forgive me there are poems at hand
first things first my selfish
schemes can wait I would never
forgive myself
                though I am afraid
hermano I have hard words for your
young ears

          This business about
taking the summer off to write
a navel ooops
the truth again as always outs
novel
          there now
Well it is

what
          Pure Kentuckiana
you are the most careful bastard

I have ever encountered more careful
than Grant C you are all so careful
It is why I left   Get your finger
out of your ass

If you will excuse
me for saying so you will someday have
to choose between being a paperboy
& a writer
& FURTHERMORE as Ezra
would say if you want to be a poet
you will have to make harder choices
still

I saw a man this morning
in Calle Sol his eyes swollen shut
from a beating   His young son
was with him hand in hand
It was impossible to tell
who was leading whom
not even they knew
I am sure

Take off from what
pray   Is writing a part of your life
or not   And a summer good God
Adams if I did not know you
to be brilliant but young
I would think you a fool
You might as well take the summer
off to play with yourself or make
mobiles for the crippled children
If you have a novel to write
you will write it & it will cost

James Baker Hall

you your life if it is worth
writing   Don't talk to me
about taking the summer
off

        Which brings me to your
poem de Soutine   Lucky you
did not try to write about Gauguin
I would come to Lexington & crack
your young head

                But even Soutine
who incidentally you vastly overrate
deserves better at least half your
mind and let's face it
a little of your heart
just a little
Billy

        Have you ever
looked at his work
I think not

                You are writing
about a man's struggle
for his integrity
& you seem hardly
aware of the fact

                skimming
surfaces you suppose compelling
like one of nature's insistent
waterbugs Leave waterbugs
to nature   You're an artist

Do you remember

                    & never
use the word rainbow again
never   Maybe in French
I don't know but you prove
no more able to restore the word
to English than Mr. Lawrence
the less said about the innocent
the better

                    I sorely mistrust
anyone who hangs carcasses
in his room to watch them rot
but I have an inkling of what
such fits are about having
specialized in them most
of my life
            But you seem
to have not the slightest
a careful Kentuckian
with his finger
missing

            If I sound intolerably
arrogant it is because I am
but this is not a matter
of taste yours mine
or anybody else's

                    I am
surely the oldest living
thirty-two-year-old
maybe the oldest

James Baker Hall

living period
Surely

What do you think
of me now Kathleen

And because I know you to be
a poet in the making one
of the two or three I have ever
known & I include all the books
in the Library of Congress
& know that you have no need
or want of delicacies
which are always lies always
leave them to your Kentuckians
& academics

I have
a 12th-century mind
best to face it

& WHATSOMORE
your handwriting is worse than
mine worse than the blind JJ
in the last mix of the Wake
Desist
What do you mean you
gave your typewriter to Ducksoo
I thought surely he would be
president of Korea by now
if not the world   What kind
of self-castration is that
You
did not want to type de Soutine

as well you shouldn't the man
sucking the artist again giving
away his typewriter indeed   Don't
tell Orphan Annie about hard times
do everything for him or nothing
rent him a typewriter & pay the rent
only don't give Mata Hari or even Ezra
your typewriter

        Maybe you should
take the summer off to write a novel
after all

      I'll get off your back
if you will you didn't lose a leg
at Argonne that's the trouble//

There is a word in Hawaiian   hanamai
it means literally work-sick
It is used with regards to fucking
mostly
      excuse me Kathleen
but equally applicable to poetry
there not being nearly as much
poetry in Hawaii as fucking
or anywhere else
      Work
until you are sick & then
work some more Billy
There is no other way
It isn't the hours
it's where the words are coming from

                              James Baker Hall

& that is not something
Grant C or this new man
Harris will tell you

                    Trust old Stanislavski
I love you well hermano but you are
a clod sometimes even
on your wedding night

This brings me to The Rope Walker
a great poem   Here you have gone in
& done your work instructed me
which is the least I expect
of you
          & moved me
which is the most

That the man who wrote
The Rope Walker wrote
in the same lifetime this
de Soutine business
boggles the mind
It is a work of near genius
there are no rainbows in it
you are writing from where
you live I honor you
You can have my typewriter anytime//

I'm not done with you yet Billy
Please stop maligning your magazine
immediately I know only too well
what the Hudson Review & those hounds

have to offer that Stylus does not
& it is why I prefer you absolutely—

Which brings me back
to my beginning
as everything seems to

                    Listen
if this sounds utterly presumptuous
just tell me I'll understand

But I thought maybe the two of you
would like to come down here
this summer
                    A honeymoon
or a vacation or however
you choose to think of it

I don't have a great deal
to offer but this is a tolerable
place one of the very few
There is sun
& beach & water
SJ itself is beautiful
the old city

            I will get you
a place you need not worry
about anything except getting here
There are two rooms vacant this moment
on the next roof top over   I can see
inside them almost as I write
Give me the word & I'll secure it

James Baker Hall

During the day
you will be left alone
strictly
        & at night we
will eat & talk & drink wine
we will read poetry to each other

        As the spirit
moves us we will take
long walks

        Just tell me
if I am a fool I will
understand

        There are even several other
people here whose company
is no more trying than my own

What do you say

You can write your novel
here Billy on my typewriter

l&k p

2.12.56/SJ

      Dear Billy Baxter Axter
il milgor fabbro lest we forget
or remember

      The garbage trucks
are whining in the streets below
the lizards hang on the window
screen in front of my face
they have followed me around
the world & found me
not wanting sly & cunning

Odysseus all sunburst & cloudfist
ruined western culture
& not even Ezra
understands it

      Listen
you constipated bugeyed
cocksucker I feel this moment
like an old San Juan whore
sequaciously into her decline
among oils & lotions
seeing the first honest smile
of a lifetime

      You are a decent
man gentle beyond imagination
I will do everything I can to justify
the trust you place in me

                James Baker Hall

                              Frankly
I thought when I dropped that letter
that I was mad on the long razor
slid back to childhood
dreams will be the death of us all
& had dignity permitted
I would have entered the chute
bellbottoms up & flapping
to retrieve it

                    It would embarrass
us all for you to know how moved
I am that you are coming here/

& since I seem intent
on speaking to you both
& despise deception especially
my own let me begin again formally

Dear Bill & Sweet Kathleen my children
of light   I am nothing if not formal
Permit me the crudity of addressing
you both in one letter
                         The truth is

The only excuse for beginning anything
again is in those words the truth is
the admission that all that has gone before
is a lie & the hope beyond all reason
that what follows will not be

                         The truth is

I have been defeated repeat defeated
for the ten thousandth time at prose
I had the innocence to try once more
to write the great American something
or other & no doubt will again I'm sure
when I know beyond even small quarrel
that I have not one whit the character
necessary for anything
but short poems very short

                    You Billy
will write the great American something
or other but I have read nothing
& never will & will end badly
adrift without friends
better than I will deserve

                    My last sentence torn
from the carriage in a yellow crumple
lying portside now reads

                    Sweetness
& light left Mudville about this time
we on its heels   Closer to the sea . . .

Isn't that just dot dot dot
My but aren't I just
dot dot dot

                    My brain unravels
in prose sentence by sentence
five pages & I'm hanging on the screen
with the lizards
                    I want desperately

James Baker Hall

my magnum opus my periplum something
Homeric & grand want nothing else
frankly

    I was born the wrong man
in the wrong time maybe I should
race sports cars or make fish nets

All things that are
are light

    But how
does one say that
in story

    Closer
to the sea
indeed

    There is no telling
is an Americanism it is the title
of a novel about America it is
a novel about America

    So that is
my fate to write the title of a novel
never to be written such a well
of light there is no
shadow nothing
can follow
only burdens

    There is no telling

there is no telling indeed closer
to the sea

     I have a theory
I doubt that it is mine but I
will claim it anyway that holds
out the possibility of a sound
for every person a kind of cosmic
auditory crosshair music of the spheres
sort of thing

       & you dissolve
on contact with your sound
dissolve nirvana

& so it must be true
that le mot juste
if it is juste enough
would dissolve everything
that went before & after

There is no telling no
telling indeed

      I know
that you think I am
rationalizing Billy
but that is all
you know/

     Enough enough
tell me to keep my defeat
to myself you are right
of course

James Baker Hall

Here I am
climbing this snake charm
of ill humor as always

Let me slide down & speak
of the poems I packed off
so brashly giving you scarce
time to breathe

        You are too kind
too kind I languish in praise
become intolerable

        And you Kathleen
are a sweet breath of light into this
grim consternation poets
among semicolons & line feeds
I shall say of Kathleen Kathleen
enmeshed Adams in what he loved
& that was speech & that was
Kathleen

        Aren't I the one
though/

        There is at hand the last
I hope of a long feather of letters
perfumed from one Warren Sams editor
of the Totem Review & he wishes
if I understand him properly
to fly all the way to SJ
to suck my cock

& I don't even
know the man   What has happened
to manners

& while most of them
are dull & literary & full of lies
he says this

I grow old I grow old
I shall wear my foreskin rolled
unquote

Kafka once said
in a letter send me a stone
for my birthday it will contain
all our love
Or was it Rilke

How is that Adams   You aren't
so goddamn smart   If you talk
like Degas you have to paint
like Degas   Not Theo's concierge
At least van Gogh believed
in God
Get out
of the university immediately
or else you will turn into a sports car
or a Presbyterian

Tell them about me
at Oxford or better Gethsemene
I have always been tempted
to become a monk will

James Baker Hall

if I don't kill
myself//

       I read
your bloody Quaker Graveyard
wait let me read it again

I was right the first time
might have known

          Frightfully
downeast extolling Boston ladies
& Constant Comment heirglooms
until I thought I would puke
He takes himself about too much
in a picnic hamper all torqued
up in the modern mode full of angst
but a picnic hamper nonetheless

as incidently you do too
Both of you want to be pitied
above all else
& of course are

I mistrust all confessions
in the name of Lowell   The man
could not be honest with himself
even if he tried
         & I give him
at least the credit not to try

Mainly the poem is music the craft

is there in rich profusion wonderful
& all that the meters and rimes
hats off
            May Allen Tate move
him from the pup tent
into the main house
forthwith
            Mainly music & good
music if a bit removed
& formal not classical
but formal

            Nonetheless the man
has written here several true lines
about the sea which I will forever
begrudge him   Until now I have never
believed that except for the fishermen
themselves the New England coast
had anything whatsoever to do
with the sea Who could look
at those houses on Cape Cod
or Cape Ann & believe otherwise
Even Plum Island which ought to have
                              a chance

but doesn't   But then
I have always been a snob
if not a fool

            If Ez Po is right
& one needs only six great lines
to become immortal then Lowell
has made it already to wit

            . . . Let the seagulls wait

James Baker Hall

For water, for the deep where the high tide
Mutters to its hurt self, mutters and ebbs.
Waves wallow in their wash, go out and out,
Leave only the death-rattle of crabs,
Sucking the ocean's side.

That is not from the picture
window or the after-dinner stroll
I would have it written on my wall
on my grave
on my chest so
don't tell me
I am not well read
you impudent bastard/

Which reminds me all this talk
of graves & the sea
One favor I am ashamed
to ask it ashamed but listen

Barbara Bradford do you know her
Taught English to illiterate freshmen
like myself when I was there & maybe
still does Well there is really
no civilized way to handle this
so what the hell here it is

We had a love affair
Barbara & I & since
I was her student &
it was most indiscreet
we let not a soul know

Even now you must not

that covey of old maid professors
would land on her jackals & magpies
promise me

So bring me word of her
will you I dare not write to her
for I am in love with her still
I write poems to her will
for the rest of my life

Isn't this
the silliest goddamn thing
you have ever heard

Go see her
for me & hold her hand ask her
about her health or the weather
or her brother

What is it
that all the women I love
have brothers they buy
sports cars for

Someone
told me she was Dean of Women
at some fancy eastern girls school
but I refuse to believe it//

Persuade your blushing bride Billy
not to use so many exclamation
points

James Baker Hall

or I will fall
upon her in a fever

Don't tell me I was young
once myself it is not
true

    l&k paul

    * * *

Kathleen Kathleen as I live
& breathe my death you are
sweet you are the one I love
you & hardly know you

The first thing I will tell
your genius husband on deplaning
is to watch you with Latin cunning
for I will find you in secret
at the first chance

        What all
your funny questions amount to
is this
    Can you live here
the way Mommy taught you

& the answer is absolutely not

There is no place like home
& no one like Mommy thank God
if you want the Brown Hotel in Louisville

then please go to the Brown Hotel
in Louisville

Come here
some other time
if you wish

There are lizards & bugs here
dirty children incurable disease
death nothing heroic that is not
essentially sad

Still
I fully expect you to depart
in finer health than you arrive
& forget about books I won't
let you read one
if you bring it

Is it not
enough to talk fish & drink
rum

I have a deep hatred
of books with which I will
infect you I am sure
& tourists
If you wear a funny hat & bring
a camera I will likely hit you
in the groin

Do women have groins

I talk to you this way because I love

James Baker Hall

you you myopic hussy
What gall
not to remember me I spoke to you
four or five times

& I can be
depended upon to do any & everything
for those I love get you
bottles of aspirin
& mosquito spray

Please
please it is all cared for food
lodging everything I have even
had the water of San Juan purified
just bring a pretty summer dress
& a bathing suit

Your lodging
consists of two rooms one for privacy
part of the house the other
like my room screened on the open roof
a vent pipe standing guard
As I write these words
I can see us at the table there
two roofs over
You can expect
a flower color of your choice
standing in the vase on your arrival

You can I
promise turn right around
& go back if you become ill
or unhappy Nothing

is inexorable no
big steps only
many small ones
No grand passions
only many sweet loves

Ah well
you are a sweet & tender young
thing of my own description
something I have never been
How am I to know what goes
through such a head

I am
used to the islands & the islanders
trust me I will hover about you
with smiles & the latest issue
of the New Yorker generally
protect you from the foggy dew

If you were my own fair bride
I would not be so solicitous
It is my belief that a woman
if she is to be lived with
must be totally disillusioned
then rebuilt with care
An idea
which has proved unworkable
to date

Don't be dull & don't
believe anything you hear

James Baker Hall

about any place or anybody
even if I say it

Yr Servant paul

* * *

I had every hope of getting out
of this alive but the truth is
no such thing is possible ever
The truth is I am almost afraid
to say anything We have all
had such good response
one to the other It is all
very good & new very exciting

The truth is I have avoided as usual
saying the one thing this letter was
meant to say

   Instead I spoke as usual
of my defeat as though it were not
inevitable & beside the point
Laid it I see now portside
at your feet Praeder
in a yellow crumple
such a pity

   Fuck the defeats
the truth is I am again suffering
them The truth is I am again
writing The truth is I cannot

tell you what your letters
mean to me
& this visit

Perhaps we are
even honest perhaps
we can purify one
another holding
our distant mirrors
up to nature &
to ourselves
I believe it

            //These poems
  then   what does one say   I began
  this letter with little else in mind
  some civilized way to put them
  into your hands
                  & tried to end it
  without even sending them
  What does one say indeed
  You are the first to see them
  not even Barbara

            I could not
  tolerate some horsesass
  at the Antioch Review
  defining himself
  in their presence

            I do hope
  you will bring word of Barbara
  it weighs into the silence at the end

James Baker Hall

of each sentence heavy among all things
I say & cannot say   I will not mention
it again cannot you must understand
It is of course no matter

They look meager enough
a few dozen lines
thirty-two years
going on sixty

I find it impossible to talk
about them to think
about them even

        I go off
in small motions
of dread
turning back
on myself
embarrassed & hurt

The one called Light
is simply the typographic
expression of dragonflies
mating over a black lake quite
beautiful

            The only hitch is
the female eats the male
for supper after love

First I called it Light
then Song #8 for Barbara
then Light again

Which I suppose come to think
of it is the story of my life

Too bad

Love to you both   paul

James Baker Hall

2.22.1956/sj

                My dear lotus
on the oblique my blossom

A letter at hand from your husband
says you are in a skunk hole & spinning
down badly to write & cheer you up

I will do no such thing   You
have slept with another man
It means nothing to me
that you are married to him
Now you must pay the price
don't expect sympathy from me
you're lucky you don't have VD

Here I sit o carib isle o sun
sequestered newly barbered
I smoke too much
& am an evil man bad
but when I smell of soaps & lotions
I could fill Carnegie Hall argue
with Schoenberg about Brahms
atonal or minor A Fully expect
in the next post a sapphire tie pin
from the Royal Family of Belgium/

Tell your doctor there that there are doctors
here civilization tissues pills
even a hospital if it will put his mind
at rest that women have children
here daily
                One of the seventeen

sufficient reasons that I would
not be a woman is that you cannot
be barbered among mirrors & straight
razors in a white cape leaned back
in a chair & spun raised and lowered
among lotions shaved among mirrors
My my
          A man of my temperament would have
a private barber

          See Praeder among
the honored dead look at him I say
look he is peaceful
in the kind light he
brings lemon drops
& seaweed he eats
fresh fruit on the flagstone terrace
he entertains his friends with madrigals
& Elizabethan chants a pavane of hawkbells
to the backing sea
Praeder

          All this reminds me
of the story of my life   Did I
ever tell you
          I ran off to Chicago
with an aesthetic bellydancer at 16
& my mommy didn't even
care

          Have you ever read
Dostoyevsky   Have you ever heard of
Dostoyevsky

James Baker Hall

I myself have read only
ten things four poems a play by Chekhov
& two by Shakespeare & three novels
But they were chosen with great cunning
& I have parlayed them into a reputation
for wide reading & meanness
ask your husband

          You/he
should never have told me
that he was out of town
I feel adulterous beware
of envy there is nothing
in the crosshatches
of the heart
so dark

          But I have just taken
a shower how can I be bad
o no how can I be sad
Dear Blossom my lotus dear
come float with me
my carib isle

          I envy all people
who can spell who have homes
& can make flashlights work
                              I hate
them of course
                    But I would change
places with my banker en moment
& he knows it & it is
intolerable

There are mountains
yes & valleys yes & one river
designed for the earthy set   Away
from the sea though I am
bored & am sure you
would be   San Juan
is teeming & varied
as they say and/but
I have paid in advance
one month for your dwellings
so you see you have no choice

I do not mean that of course
Tell me if it will not do to be
so close
            Even as I type these words
I'm watching for your arrival in the late
afternoon   I can see the lizards on your screens
without the aid of binoculars   Tell me if this alarms you
& I will rent St. Croix//

            I have written
all this under abiding pressure
I keep looking at how much I have
& saying is that enough
is that enough
can I tell now

            For you see
I am shaved & showered
in celebration   The editor
of the Antioch Review one

James Baker Hall

Miller Thorp has seen fit
to accept one of my poems
for publication in his magazine
There it is out in all its blushing
intensity I have been dissolved
all day
with joy
I am a child at heart
younger than Billy forgive
me
    I am sure now to be rich
& famous   Will you still love me

       Your doctor sounds like all
of Lexington to me   He should live
at least half the year with his plumbing
out of doors

       Does Billy still like
Ernest Hemingway   Can you explain that
I cannot I assure you don't worry
He is not the gifted stylist that even
his detractors claim & I say that never
having read a word he has written

When I tell you not to trust me
I mean it absolutely I have
a breadstick up my nose

       Are you sure
that you are married to this man not
just living with him temporarily
I refuse to believe it

There is an old
fool who lives outside the walls here
SJ La Marina they call him Poeta
because he speaks to the empty air
& recites portions of books
the tobacco trade once paid him
to read to the workers
                    Imagine
that will you
            A particularly vile
drunkard now the trade gone
& with it his job no need
for a reader of the classics
or the alabaster of rhyme

& what oh what would America
be like if the classics
had a wide circulation
well it troubles my sleep

& so he stands in the middle
of the street when the cantinas
are closing La Poeta
reading from an imaginary book
& the children have at him
& rightly so he has outlived
his art damn him
it will never
happen to me
not today

        Do you I say
do you smell as good as I do

James Baker Hall

my sweet moving among your Gimbel's
& Macy's a snapdragon sprouting
from your nostril
                    But then it is
a foolish question no one smells
as good as I do today not even you
Nicean bark supple & knowing so full
of life tssh tssh

            You are absolutely
right about Grant C he is not ⟶
but rather ⟨⟩⟨⟩

                    Too bad
But I love him nonetheless
Did you know that he is vain
about having three male children
It is true
            It is also true
that there are worse things
in this world than vanity
his my own or anybody else's/

Here's the woe tale our fates
send me to tell you
to wit to woo

            God knows
if there had been another place
in all that fetid neighborhood
to get a cup of coffee after eight
I would never have gone there

I knew the minute I sat down
that she would . . .
                    well excuse me
I have no heart for this really
I fear I have no heart
                    The minute
you say she you know what is in store
if not this week then the next
or the next
                    It loves to happen

The Toddle House it was called
on Euclid there as I remember
across from the theater   I was no
child God knows not that I ever was
I had spent long years already
& no small expense of spirit
in the service of my country
in communications as we say
The military is much maligned
& it should not be no it allowed me
years in the Caribbean one of the few
tolerable places left   What
I was doing in Lexington Kentucky
in a university no less remains
to this day a mystery though surely
it had something to do with my dear
brother who was determined to live there
because of his wife I think
                    Wherever
whenever determination is involved
there is always a wife in it somewhere
always
                    Excuse me my sweet but this

James Baker Hall

is the story of my life you have a right
now that I am in love with you
to know
                When on entering
& taking a stool I saw her in all white
behind the counter reading
Death in Venice
                I knew
she would break my poor back
probably before morning   The Brothers K
perhaps or even Ulysses or the Tempest
but Death in Venice what can one say
Lie there my art
indeed
            Her name you won't believe this
was Shelley & she was by her own confession
a student at the university & a lover
of horses & dulcimers
                        Aren't we all
I had no more gotten to bed
that very night than she was
at the door   Stood there
on the porch in her hooded
raincoat & said not a word
She was putting herself
through school which was
infinitely more than I could say
for myself & I am sure that if I
saw her again today I would be moved
all over again even to tears
                        I fucked her
on the basin in the bathroom
& had to watch myself in the mirror
the whole time which served me right

as I always do
                It Loves to Happen
is the name of such stories   Once
you start there is absolutely no way
to stop   She wanted me to believe along
with her that all the world's universities
& dulcimers had been mere preparations
for our meeting which of course I did
why not they probably were   We
managed in our extremity to turn
the water on in the basin which she
made much of in her poems   She was
determined to talk afterwards
There was nothing I could do
there was nothing either of us
could do there never is
& she was still there
the next morning curled
up beside me with her arm
across my chest & her raincoat
in the middle of the floor
There was no way to get out
of bed without waking her
One's whole life is unavoidable
in the flowered wallpaper
of rented rooms   She was
guess what having an affair
with her writing teacher
which as you can probably see now
brings the point of this sordid tale
a little closer   I had never met
the great man & suddenly
there we were Grant C
the poor fellow

James Baker Hall

in his jealousy wanted
to send all five of my poems
to Karl Shapiro at Poetry magazine
& I had been in town only a few weeks
I apologized to everyone incessantly
offered to join the CG again anything
but they insisted   I was flattered
would be again no doubt & wrote three pages
of a novel which only made matters worse
It was I blush to remember
about wild boars in the Hawaiian forest
primeval & the flowered wallpaper
of rented rooms
                    The one unforgiveable
thing about decent people is that
they insist   They wanted to meet
their class at my place   He was
one of the three decent men
I have ever known a fool
let it be said & a teacher of writing
surrounded by young women named Shelley
I owed him nothing but I will never
forgive myself
                    We sat there all
of us on the floor drinking cheap
wine from paper cups & listened
to her read a story called Pegasus
which was not as he & the rest assumed
about him but about me   He did nothing
to deserve that   After those sessions
he would take her back to her place
& they would do whatever they did
before he went home to his wife
& children & she would hurry

back to my place wet
& horny
　　　　She was the young lady
perhaps the only person I have ever known
more vile than I but then she had the excuse
of her age   I often wonder what
has happened to her   She is married
to a denist & sports car enthusiast
I am sure lives one is invited to imagine
in a suburb torn between her children
& her lost adventure
　　　　　　　　titillated
from time to time perhaps by the poetry
of Li Po   Aren't we all

So there you have it
Praeder at his celebration
& can either of us say
that we are glad
I will never ask you
what you think
　　　　　I promise

I grow old I grow old
I need a drink

Will fold this neatly & take it
with me to the post office
You will write won't you
All good things begin & end
in the post office at night
late at night & it is late
now my sweet the post office

　　　　　　　　　　　　　　　　James Baker Hall

24/7 troubles my sleep   See me
peering into my box a hand shading
my eyes   I like envelopes
with barber poles around the edges
periplum
        I go to pieces

I leave my room now
but I will be true
to you fear not

Write to me soon

Yours with gusto

paul

   ///Grant says
that he knows one thousand things
& I believe it If he doesn't
who does

      If you drive
to Miami & stay with my brother
you can put the bloody car on blocks
in his garage for the whole month
What is it about cars or is it
the people who own them
         He
has nothing to show for his life
but a garage   Make him
do the work he is a disgrace

to the name
            Or in the back
yard with a plastic cover
or in the front better
It would serve you all right
Are you sure that you can live
four plus weeks without your car
without your mother
                  & another
word about money I will return
your letters unopened   The CG
covers me continually with dollars
I have no time to spend it all

I could write upon this all night
have absolutely no sense
of proportion
or tact

      Good night again
my sweet   All that stands
between us is your husband
whom I admire beyond measure
a better man in each & every way
for certain

James Baker Hall

4.14.56/San Juan PR

Dear Bill and Kathleen

I have written you two letters
and just threw away the second

Allow me this silence
I am desolate of late

You sound sad
            Don't come
if you have no heart
for the trip Billy
I will understand

If school and directions
fill up your life then
join school and directions
by all means

            The rest
is none of my business

I have little to offer
really aimlessness
and occasional articulation
very occasional

            Come only
on impulse for that is
my way and the way
I admire in others
Worry about anything

but accommodations
please they will be
fitting

       You can stay
in the hospital
if you wish

p

James Baker Hall

4.22.56/Calle Sol SJPR

Well as I live & breathe
you are the one both
my Billy my Lotus

   I spin in the air
above your heads light
& cunning
    Hellow there
hellow there indeed
now listen Billy

you have written a good poem
yet another as usual I am
rolled over on my back feet
in the air with admiration

But you are too smart for your own
good I am sure of it Do you know
what I mean

    In Washington there is
a museum which is better than most
not I think because of the paintings
they hold but because of the man
who hangs them You must go there
immediately if possible this very day
for they have finally shown El Greco
for the fraud he is

     A man of no true
feeling of large & suave gesture
theatrical in the worst sense broad

& unclean & facile
             & worse
an evil man for he purports
to be religious Toledo
& saints & light aspiring
faces to the blue heavens
God in the backstays of the sun
topaz cloudfists
                I hate the man
intensely

       If I ever have children
I will permit them to play in the street
& talk to strangers & pick mushrooms
but never to look at El Greco without me
present

      & so in Washington
some curator all he did
was hang him next to Goya

& that is that

No arrows no critics
in the wings no whispers

But there it all is
Next to Goya the man
is undone
revealed
       You want
to make holes
in the canvas

James Baker Hall

hang him
in tar

        You are not El Greco surely
if delivering newspapers has done nothing
else it has kept you modest
                            any more
I suspect than you could become Goya
or would want to for that matter

But five lines often are enough
if you pay for them n'est-ce pas
You carry around too many words
in your mouth Billy
& they come out too easily
you are brighter than you are deep
in this poem which is not you
Ask uncle Paul the smartest
man alive

        You ain't
holy & surely I ain't
holy
        but good poetry can be

Throw the impostors out all the old turds
& never write a poem
you don't absolutely
have to

        And drink
at least one glass
of milk every day

I could be wrong
but I am not/

        & now to Kathleen
my dear mystery I think of my own
young bride whenever I address you
it is time I married & had a son
Younger than you shy & younger
than anyone
          So that her soul
will take its shape in my person
& save us both anguish
              Young
& in love with the sea one
who laughs & cries
but not all the time

Do you know the kind
It is little enough to ask

I have lived too long in rented rooms
I have lived too long

            I see my bride
at the kitchen table loving & tender
she types my work & spells the words
properly puts in all the commas
I like her already

           I have a lung
as of today is what I want to say
& I fully intend to horrify B
by insisting that you dive

              James Baker Hall

to one hundred feet
foetus & all

That will deepen him
I dare say

        There is room
for a woman in a poet's life
in his language as long as she
bears him sons
& is as sweet
as Kathleen as healthy
as prudent
& brave

        I distrust
the whole sex of course
love only
        dot dot dot//

The truth is my dear friends
I have been sitting here some time
now having written myself
into the desolation
of that construction

I LOVE ONLY

& what pray
does one say then
what indeed

It is I fear
a long life
to be dealt with
day by day eyes
close in look not
back or to the future
be still neat
in small hopes

Already I can see my last
years friendless &
wandering
            I refuse to believe it

But the equal truth is
my dear Bill & Kathleen
& I will not darken it further

Your letter brought me back
from the dead

I cannot believe
you are coming

I have looked on it
with such odd extravagance someone
to talk to
to walk with

I have too much time to think
& not heart enough
to sustain myself

James Baker Hall

I am grateful thank you thank you

& I refuse to allow my gloom
on us one more minute you are coming
that is all that matters

I celebrate with a poem
about down tides & recognitions
what else & women how could it not be
about women elliptical & enigmatic
as love
             Having conceived of such silence
             deep her eyes & receptive
             I come
             to her small love

             & a teacup
             in the pig's ass curl
             of her little soul
             I have never conceived
             of such

& what do you think of them
apples my friends I promised you
a poem & you see what happened
I always keep my promises
Forgive me
             Put in your own lines
& semicolons do it yourself
poetry I couldn't

             en tiemp p

* * *

You said nothing of my songs
for Barbara   I do my best
& what the fuck do I care
if you like it or not
Just so if anyone asks you
the scheme of the work
is the Roman liturgy
more intricate than Dante
& Ezra

How do you like that
for knees and elbows

I heard from Grant C he dead
& I truly regret
I cannot help him
I have tried

I have lost everything
suddenly
   Should shut up
don't know how

    You must act
I know you must act now
or the jimjams will swallow
you
  Act & hate

That is important
     Without hate
civilization would not exist
life would be impossible

James Baker Hall

You think you know
but don't

　　　My hands
go to pieces I know more
of the jimjams than any one
alive
　　　& much else besides

Grunts & fardels paul

TWO

5:05 am
6.13.56/SJPR

Bill

I will slide this under your door
on my way to the base   If Kathleen intercepts it
that is no great matter   It will save me the trouble
of writing to her separately
which I can't attempt until
late tonight

       I trust
that it was clear to all parties
on the steps a couple of hours ago
that our plans for dinner together
tonight are canceled

       A big mistake
has been made I fear many little ones
will get dumped in on top of it every time now
we get together   Clarity on this
is of utmost importance to me to all of us
though I speak only for myself of course
and hope that you and your bride
will do likewise

       A hangover
actually helps otherwise
I might act as I too
often have   To please

We take off our sweaty blouses in SJ
we push the piano away from the wall

we shoot craps we stay up all night
the CG is full of questionable people
the islands full of questionable places
We end up dancing drunk too often
saying and doing things inadmissable
come daylight
             Forgetfulness
may be man's sole virtue
Forget it Billy
Okay

I don't blame you caro
If I had your bride for my own
I would be worse company than you
if such is imaginable   She asks a lot
your young lady & it's not as apparent
as she seems to think what right she has
to ask for more than a little
her distress notwithstanding
Bossiness knows only itself
& can't learn   Coupled with youth
it's ugly company & exhausting
A leading-role mentality
needs a good script

She has attributes
but self-knowledge
isn't among them
I feel for you

       Look last night
could happen again I wouldn't promise
that it won't even if I could   Fear

                                        James Baker Hall

is one thing worry another   Worry
is an ass wart hermano
painfully located
I'm not your baby sitter
I'm not your bride's baby sitter
Nor am I the messenger of your fitful union
once this note is finished

                         Your fitful union
distressed me at first now it bores me
The idea of three more weeks of it
takes hold of me first in the sphincter
& that's the easy part

                         Our situation
terrifies me frankly it exhausts me

You should have gone on back to your place
Billy my boy   You were a thankless piece of work
hovering around the door generally
being put upon
                         You have a talent for it
the power of one who truly believes
in being wronged

Have you considered going back to Lexington
with or without your bride
I think you should
Consider it I mean
Don't tell me it's impossible
The list of impossibilities
is too long already

If you're worried about Kathleen
and what she'll do
you ought to be
I am
She is

A child is a lot to get used to
I'm sure of it
it may be impossible
but leave me out of it
okay   I'm providing her
with similiar instructions

She says that she wants you to leave her alone period
that she has tried on numerous occasions to communicate
this to you and that you refuse to understand
She says that she'll take up speaking with you
again when she sees fit

I promised her like the fool I am
that I would relay this message

I don't want to hear your side of the story
I didn't want to hear hers
I never will
It's just the kind of guy I am

We'll get through this
If you need money
I've got money

I'll feel something for you again
& maybe even you for me

James Baker Hall

I'm not counting on it though
I'm counting on you Billy

p

* * *

Irritation and impatience aren't feelings
they're spleen blocking the heart
You are too young to be this far from home
& it's all my fault
                    I'm sorry

Everything I say to you
is what I refuse to know
about myself
                    & I don't have the excuse of youth

6.29.56/SJPR

Billy

Maybe she fucked somebody
maybe she didn't
Maybe it was me
maybe it wasn't
I would tell you if I knew

You think this is bullshit
because you don't know any better
These are the facts as uncle Paul
knows em

        Don't ask me
to account for her whereabouts
I was on duty   Yes
she wanders all over
that's my impression
Alone as far as I know

Only a week & a day left Billy
& we'll be shut of each other
I have no advice for you
me or her

        Yes she is
going to keep the child
That's what she's led me
to believe   More
I don't know
You think
that I do

James Baker Hall

but I don't Yes I will talk with you
Frankly I'm surprised that you want to
Call me at the base later this morning
We'll meet at the bahia bench & go
to that cafe I keep telling you about

Just skip the Saturday spear fishing
                                        okay
do everybody a favor

                        I'd skip it myself
if I thought my presence wasn't necessary
Doc doesn't know half what he thinks
he knows about the lung and about barracuda

                        You could have had relief
at the oars by asking for it Bill
and you knew it   I volunteered
twice myself   Doc volunteered
You were in love
with your blisters

I know you're hurting
I'm doing what I know to do
Of course it's not enough

p

THREE

8.22.56/SJPR

            /&&&/ my mind is
a barber pole my soul
the sea
            dear Billy
what have we here

I feel better than I ought today
mistrust me

                  Okay sonofabitch
I know that everything you say
is true everything
you have ever said
& I'll type not one more
buddenbudden & sea snort
until I have reworked it//

Later much later   There
that's better
                  or worse
don't say a word to me
I've had enough sly smiles
to last a lifetime

                  Poetry is
time   We try hard   It makes no
difference in the end /

                  Listen
I am behind myself there is
news   I have a fine new apt

Doc & I do near the Cafe Bahia
as a matter of spiritual fact
not six ax handles from the place
on the wall where we all sat
that eve viewing the stilly
deep

  I might be too old
for a roommate I might be
too old for everything
We will see
    If I can
tolerate anyone if anyone
can tolerate me it is Doc

He is forever embarrassed
about his car on the day
of your departure asks me
to apologize again ///

  * * *

Listen Billy I know but little
of your marital anguish only
what my selfishness had to know
while you were here   It would
take me years to approach the first
nuance I am sure & life is
sad enough as it is

You have more to learn
from Grant than you know
Don't throw him aside
because the new man Harris

           James Baker Hall

is the better writer
or invites you to his house
for steak & wine
You will regret it
                    We all
do the best we can
& it is not good enough
nowhere near
                    Life
defeats me daily & with ease
I am sorry but certain facts
are inconsolable
                         Age
will bring you to this
unless fear keeps you
a child

        And since I seem to be
in the mood let me instruct you
in yet another matter   Send
your poems to Karl Shapiro
at Poetry magazine or I will
crack your vain young head   You
want to break into print
without help well how precious
can you get more precious
than I bless you   That is not
real pride Billy   You distress
me at times make me think you will
end up in New York or San Fran
among the literati after all
Hudson smudson you snob publish
where you are wanted preferably
among friends

Well well caro
I can withhold no longer I see
now where all this is a-leading
The truth is that Lil sent some
of my things to W.C. Williams
the sheaf she took back with her
& the old fuck liked them
In fact wrote me the kindest letter
I have ever received ever will
said that the Songs for Barbara
are "major work"
Can you believe it
I am dissolved
in gratitude
& confused

I reread him
wanting my mind changed
but it wasn't   Kindness
makes great poetry unattainable
though he certainly does more
by it than most

            Not a word
from Ezra I should have known
better

        Write to me sweetheart
I perish without attention

l&k P

James Baker Hall

9.3.56.SJPR

Dear Adams
Dear Harris

You are right
of course
but give me
time I need
time

I hate
you both

Gene Autry

9.26.56/SJPR

Dear Billy   If you please
hold on to your hate whoops
hat   Hold on to your hat
for there is absolutely no way
. . . dot dot dot

        Well indeed
I embarrass myself time
& again

      You would think
I was Shelley with her legs
spread mounting
a horse-hugging story
called Pegasus

        All this frenzy
twinkletoes initialing the sky
light get a hold of yourself
Praeder is based on the notion
that I must plunge in & tell
you straightway that I have
just come back from Atlanta
where I gave a poetry reading
Don't act as though you are not
impressed

      So you will excuse
my long silence   Or perhaps not

It was Miller whatshisname's doing
I should be indebted to him

James Baker Hall

for life probably will be
Robert Lowell wasn't there
but everyone else was I am
sure   From the names I recognized
I concluded that everyone there
was Somebody which I am sure
they were & that were I not
the perverse circuitous
sonofabitch that I am
I would have enjoyed
being among the chosen
Lest you think I have lost
the last trace of sanity I was
one third of an hour & a half
program of the young & unheard of
the other two thirds of which were
indeed young   I never felt so old
in all my life   &&&
well the thought of them
makes murder in me
they were merely young
I am sure but
I seem to have lost
all patience

            I read tolerably
well considering & am still
unknown though not as young
as I used to be never was
I left convinced of one thing
that either I change my name
to Randall Ciardi or I will never
get my poems published forget
the opera   There was a fellow

there by the name of Snodgrass
a poet fill in the blanks
& he was kind enough to take
a cc of Calle Sol back
to the university of somewhere

Has a friend who writes music
Don't we all //

        The truth is
I met a man there who claimed
to know Barbara said she
had married a reverend
& was leaving the academy
I refuse to believe it
I had fully intended to read
my songs but I could no more
have read them no nada
nada y puis nada

We are all too sensitive
to be alive

        I am cursed
with the ability to see
myself clearly
from time to time

Unavoidably we meet ourselves
in dirty rooms lying awake
on a sprung bed where
we are forgotten

James Baker Hall

& can forget
nothing
          It is not worth it
it is not worth anything
In the struggle to find a shred
of ourselves in the tangle of days
& nights we are painfully
all eyes painfully
Everyone we know
walks across the flowered wall
across the ceiling we could never
touch them   We can never
touch them

          //But all is not
lost you constipated old pearl
diver I have been waiting
the while to tell you this
a pox on you & Harris
for I sent the Mar sequence
to Shapiro hoping that he would take them
& give me the prize thus confounding
you both you overweaning fascist
pricks & he did
          So are you
confounded & such
as you ought to be

All this reminds me somehow
Carla del Ponte of Weimaraner
fame she calls daily
to inquire of you   She

was charmed out of her mind
Billy what did you do all
those times at the cabana
what did you do
              She pretends
to be interested in Kathleen too
but clearly you have seized her
heart
        What should I invest her
with next time   Cunning words
of my own choice

                  Advice
is useless projection malo
moon shine in the dirt never
take it especially from me
                        So here
is my advice   Why don't you get
out of Lexington

                    Tell me I know
not what I say & it is true
but the truth is
the truth is
...

                  I'll stop
that is the only decent
thing to do & I am nothing
if not decent nothing
indeed

The final truth is
there is no disorder

James Baker Hall

but it takes a saint
nothing less
              The waves
have mercy the rocks no
mercy at all
              You're the waves
Billy as you always have been
Suck it up is what waves do

              I would send you
my hawkbell mi poeta had it
sufficient character

amor   p

* * *

Doc got his leg scraped up
by a mako shark is
insufferable about it

10.17.56/SJPR

Dear Bill/

Things go badly
with me
I have nothing
to share
& love
no one

This is why
you & I
quarreled here

I am empty

not shallow
but empty

And so will you be
in a few years

I heard about
you & Kathleen
sorry

Get an older chick
next time

           Few women
understand anything
but the more age
they acquire the more

James Baker Hall

they learn to look
sweet wise & helpful
quietly

Maybe your heart
is broken
if so I am
sorry

love & kisses P

11.7.56/SJPR   /Dear Billy

I got them off to Ellman
the Songs for B the long Moro Castle
everything on your generous list
I am getting a hide in my old age
keep surprising myself
& heard third hand they have reached
the great man's desk
                    I thank you

I believe not one minute
in this sort of thing
of course
          At times I am
so fraudulent I can scarcely
conceive of myself

                  Shapiro
took not only the Mar poems
but get this followed immediately
by accepting Calle Diablo & another
I can't recall at the moment which
one a Song for guess who
What do you think
of your uncle Paul now
sweetheart

          Looks like
I will be in the East before long
Washington or New York I put in
for a transfer don't ask me
to explain

James Baker Hall

I will go to St. Thomas
for three weeks before I leave
or maybe three hours I wish
we could have gotten over there
while you were here & to St. Croix
I'm often reminded
in this part of the world
of a university library
                              splendor
taken over by the wrong
people
            It makes the ruined magnificence
of San Juan agreeable indeed

                        //Listen about Harris
I don't know   The man writes too much
you know Writes with a capital W
The things you sent are very good
& all that   I'm impressed   But then
I get the feeling that I am supposed to be
You say he is for real a poet
& I trust you absolutely
in such matters but I will have
to see more first okay

                        Look again
mira it is none of my business
obviously but things are as bad
as they seem they always have been
& I would not for one minute
deny it but
they cannot

after all
get worse

That sounds I am sure
like the sophistry
of a brittle soul
but it is not
As you grow & grow
older you will come
into it with relief

The truth is your letter
it has moved me deeply
You are suffering
I am sorry
            But
there is no way
around it
        not if you want to be
a man & not if you want
to write poetry

            Writing
is no answer but when you feel
deeply there is little else to do

What you say now
is of no importance
A real affection
is rising
in you

    There are men
around me daily who have at life

James Baker Hall

& have at women & they
are nothing

It is the quality
of the affection that matters
the only thing
You know that
better than I

Tragedy/Women
Love/Children
Fuck them all
Billy
Leave them to men
whose eyes have not been torn
out of their heads
by what they have seen

You may not
believe this you may not be ready
to believe this yet/still
in your suffering you
have made yourself responsible
to the empty air
to God
to the world
it is all the same

Men & women
may love you
but you cannot
love them
no matter
how you try

& it will
in time
kill you

All that you
can have & it is
by no means certain
that you will attain it
is greatness a great
spirit
& agony will
in time have no meaning

The poet is the proud snail Billy
We watch him for the whaleroads
he makes on stone & concrete
The waving stalks
of his eyes
in the early light
The rhythmic contractions
of his slimy sidelit body
The colorful wakes
of his secretions

///Your letter & the prize money
from UK came in the same mail
with a letter from my brother damn
his comfortable soul   I cannot
respect comfortable men
like him & neither
I suspect can you
henceforth
It constitutes

James Baker Hall

a loss to owe nothing
to anyone you know that
of course but only loss
teaches
      The rest
is merely thought
the less of it the better

       For christsakes
man don't be idle I am encouraged
in my own work by yours don't want
your stimulation to stop

If it kills you
too bad

l p

9.2.57/D.C.

Well Querido Primo—

                    Howl
is here & the Evergreen Review
& I thank you   There is a good deal
to be said for these Beat writers
They want polish which no doubt
their program will make difficult
but I salute them   The alternatives
are so dreadful   Have a look
at this new anthology edited
by Hall Pack & Simpson
Poetry may be too tenuous
already to withstand the influence
of all these professors & students
yourself notwithstanding Billy
Tell me I know nothing of what
I speak it is always true//

So much has happened since I last
wrote as they say fill in the blanks
I was in Lexington a few weeks ago
shortly after you left for the coast
& I saw Grant & Kathleen's family
                              & your son
Kathleen was in Bloomington already///

I have been sitting here
for a lifetime stopped
at that last sentence

James Baker Hall

Surely I had more in mind
than facts facts
interest me not
at all I know as few
as humanly possible
& forget those as soon as possible

But Lexington puts an end
to thought
        Comfort
has its final say there
the daytime mind runs the show
is the show Transport
has no chance none
I am glad you are out

                /I spent ten days
two days maybe it was only
four minutes on a fishing boat
out of St. Thomas before I left
a lifetime at least one
I almost jumped

Remind me to tell you
about it
someday

        /When in Lex I saw
Barbara   Well there it is out
& I'm glad & the truth is
I still love her always
have always will
Whatever that means

I told her
of my literary successes
& she cried

I don't know
how to explain this
or anything else
I don't understand
anything that happens
especially between men
& women

She did marry a reverend
it lasted not a month
was annulled
I asked no questions
there are no answers
anyway

I was delighted
& relieved to see
her   Can you believe it
I am sure you can

/I've been having an affair
with a woman from Cleveland
doesn't that sound shitty
I moved into a new apartment
last week to escape her but
it didn't work nothing ever does
She was here in fact when your letter
arrived breaking my back
with protestations & prostrations
She wants to move in with her guitar

James Baker Hall

& potter's wheel   Every man does
the best he can   She has me nailed
to the floor the ceiling I feel
like a Godless Chagall
in glossy black & white

Your comments about love
made me sigh

          The grand passion
is not for me really
or anyone else
          To hold
hands & be quiet is
enough
          When the passion
is grand it is not
the woman you love
it's yourself

          /Listen
if I cannot go to France
October next I will try
to visit you in SFran okay
Have you wowed them I dare say
What is there in the lit life
beside Howl & how is westcoast
pussy
          Forgive me I seem intent
on being a fool this morning

The academy is yours
if you want it I am sure
I told Bracket in no jest

that you would amount
to something pick
your mark

     I had great ideas
of joining the literary world here
I seem never to tire of hope bless me
I would have a paper route
if I didn't need my sleep but
I insulted everybody I met
immediately & probably won't be
Poetry Consultant
after all

     I accepted
to my everlasting shame
an invitation to meet along
with several other "new talents"
with Randall whatshisname
at the Library of Congress
the one with the love-40 beard
this is the way the world ends
with Randall in his Mercedes Benz
& we hated one another instantly
He wished to know my favorite
translation of Rilke
So there I sat
at a round table
with four other fools
& said not a word
until finally I made the manners to leave

     So much for the literary
world in Washington   Harris's friend

James Baker Hall

Rosenbaum was another order decent
enough but he is busier than Lyndon Johnson
persuading the Japanese to forget that we
dropped atomic bombs on them   I must write
& thank Harris   Let's hope that I will

I bought a camera last week
isn't that what you are supposed
to say when the Japs are mentioned
Well I did & I'm glad   When we visit
I will make the dust jacket picture
for your first novel that way
my name will accompany yours
into immortality///

There is something the matter
with this letter I know not
what there is something
the matter with me I know
not what there is something
the matter
        I bore myself
& others

       I am trying
to write a poem about
my father   You didn't know
I had a father
did you

      Neither did I
No wonder I cannot write
the poem

Your son
looks like you mira
you will forgive sentiment
among old friends

            That frankly
as I am sure you know is why
I spoke of my father of course
there is no such person so that
I could speak of your son you
must forgive me
                This & everything
Of course you won't & shouldn't
but you must

            I have faith
in you that is no bullshit
You are an artist
I am not

But think more about your personal
person Billy
Give up
& then write

cårinos paul

//There is a fellow here
who has a million dollars
to start an advertising firm
offers me 20 thou a year plus

James Baker Hall

to join   That's a lot of money
I wish it were less

    * * *

I seem to want to mention my book
as though you knew about it
You should hate me
for not telling you
I won't let you not
I thought you would be jealous
which is all about me not you caro
Well there it is   I'm ashamed
thank God   Who would have thought
I had it in me

There's this small press in Atlanta
a three-person operation
they want to publish a book
of my poems
                "whenever I'm ready"
I will call it Songs for Barbara
They do handsome bookmaking
The man in charge is perfectly sincere
& intelligent   My poems
are all he knows about me
all he wants to know
                Still
I can't seem to rouse my spirit
to the occasion

        This thing

about my father
It's the one story
I have to get to
if I'm ever to write
another poem & I'm helpless
There are no words
within hearing

James Baker Hall

FOUR

10.5.57/D.C.

Dear Bill

      I cannot tell
what time is the right time
or which words carry best

The fact is Kathleen and I
were married a few days ago

Somehow we both expected this
in a strange and unsaid way

Very well   It is a fact
I ask your indulgence

No one knows of this yet
just the immediate immediates
We will live in Washington

More than this is perhaps
only talk
         for small mouths
small hours

            Between men
in matters of moment etc
I believe simplicity
is desirable

      I could
scarcely say I am not
anxious to hear

your comment
Perhaps you are
the only person
I will ask
for an opinion

Very well again very well

If I sound dreadfully final
about all this it is because
having reached deep now into
my thirty-third year I
am not lightly committed
to this marriage
and being so accustomed
to light commission
I stand in danger
of taking too much
grim determination
into it

     I wish merely
to live with Kathleen
and of course the young man
and to try for the stability
I have so far not achieved

Yes certainly
I am too grim

        //I should shut up
now & send this I know that
& you know I know it but

James Baker Hall

it's like everything else
I know useless

I sent your fine new poem
to Karl S. about a week ago no
almost two with a letter trying
to say simply 'here is a poem'
It was nothing fancy nothing
you would not have approved of
You know how refractory he can be
sometimes   I hope he likes the poem
He has your address and mine   I hope
he lets us both know
what is what soon /

Maybe a short letter now
is best

Certainly
there will be a period
of readjustment and you
are part of it

I await your answer
hopefully

It is not so much
what you say
but what you finally
come to think
that is important to me

One expects
politeness   We are all

gravely polite
even Spanish
in this respect at times
I think K & I will be happy

Let me hear

love Paul

* * *

Galley proofs
of Songs for Barbara
are in the works
so I'm told

James Baker Hall

10.21.57/Washington

Dear Billy

      Thanks and so on
for your good understanding

There are by the way just
the two of us at the moment
As soon as we find an apartment
suitable Kathleen and I will drive
over to Lexington and pick up
the young man
and whatever gear she thinks necessary
This week she is in Lexington by herself
for reasons best understood
by a woman
Making circles
I suppose
before lying
down

      She
asks that nothing
be said for a week or so
which I don't understand
but which is a small matter
whatever it signifies
and I do everything
I am asked

      So again
your indulgence please

A life time
is very bloody long
and a week or so
doesn't matter to me
one way or the other//

What do you think
of my eventual adoption
of your son

I do think
it probably best
for the young man
especially when he starts school etc

    Let me know
how you feel
about this
and if all is
agreeable
I will proceed
with the necessary
papers etc

    Lawyers
doctors generals
the professionals
of this world
strike terror
in me

    O by the way
Kathleen withdrew from Indiana

James Baker Hall

and from the academy in general
for at least the next few years
I am very pleased at this

Love Paul

* * *

Let me hear something
I think of you more often
than you might imagine

5.12.58/Washington D.C.

Come now WBA relax

My silence has been part sloth
& part plan
            which I suppose
is the story of my life

The plan part was to permit
the principals ie Kathleen
her mother you
& the young man
                        to jog
around to your own
separate ways
of allowing
a new player

            Maybe I
was just plain shirking
my family duties
but maybe not

                  The money
decision is not my sole
province not that I do not
subscribe to Kathleen's position
that is not the question rather
that this and other matters
are rightfully to be considered
jointly
            formerly by Kathleen
and her mother now by Kathleen

James Baker Hall

and myself
                    Your $25 check
by the way cleared
the second time around
and something called a stroller
was purchased by Kathleen

I hope the Bank of America
con California has not thrown
you into a white stucco jail
or empounded your typewriter
In the future do not hesitate
to ask for consideration
in such matters   Both
Kathleen and I understand
about graduate student wages
We are not so needy
that arrangements
cannot be made

                    It seems unavoidable
that money will have to be discussed
from time to time among other
sobrieties
                    And I wish
to do it openly   I will not
trust the uncle cg to support
us forever I assure you

It is unfortunate that we
both are for the time being
without the necessary cash/

Here is the letter from KS

about your poem   It is not
discouraging I think   He is
an honest man would not say
that he is interested in your
work if he is not

                    And the copy
of my galley proofs you requested
I see them from time to time lying
about the apartment here
& fall
into utter
confusion

That this marriage
& this book
come to me
together
make portent
beyond my poor mind
Terrify me

Love Paul

* * *

Kathleen has contacted her lawyer
in Lexington and he will have
the adoption papers
drawn up shortly

James Baker Hall

3.3.60/NYC

Dear Bill

      Forgive me
this scrawl but
I've put this off
too long already

About the young man
can we wait

I am in mid
air suspended
the dark
vast & middle

I'm worse company than usual

The time is not right
there is too much
that is new
adjustments
must be made
more time
is needed

I think we all need more
time

      Kathleen is young
& easily frightened
I swore that I would never
again live in NYC

There are times
when I understand everything
times when I understand nothing

//The Avenue is not as bad
as I imagined   I meet
serious people daily
I hope before long
to get back to my own
writing
        Though I am
past the point
where I think
it matters

        Kathleen
and the young man
are well

    The baby is
recovering from a cold
her first of the season

Thank you for your
thoughtfulness //

        Each year
I think that if I can just
get through the winter
sanity will return

James Baker Hall

but of course
it never does

love & kisses paul

12.22.61/New York City

Dear Bill

      Kathleen and I
have talked it over
         Which
must be the shittiest way
in the world to begin
a letter
      And we
have decided that you
should send no more money
She will cash this last check
and then that will be the last

I have a job and I am ashamed
to say how much money I am making
and it seems a fair bet now
that I can keep it or get
a better one

      I always
suspected that I would end up
selling scented soap to housewives
It is why I could never kill myself
I make no apologies for Madison Avenue
it is every bit as awful as rumored worse
but there are a few souls around not in league
with the devil

      There is no
reason for you to believe

                  James Baker Hall

a word I say I certainly
do not

A friend
of a friend is setting
Moro Castle to music
It will be performed
at Brandeis University
in Boston   So I am told//

I have a study
in the attic   We live
in last century elegance
here on Staten Island
but children what can one say
they are largely unforgiveable
especially my own

The young man is
well and happy enough
I think   Kathleen is
a decent mother
a very good one
in fact her bossiness
fits the job description

The trouble
with a study is
it reminds one
and after a certain age
one should not be
reminded

I used to believe
a lot of things
the ham red sun
& I still do
I still do

I am sorting
old letters
& broken ideas
cleaning up
my study forgive
my confusion

Forgive me

//I have an idea for a film
an inverted Christ story
done in cowboys & indians
If I get enough money behind it
would you be interested
                          Don't
turn up your nose at films
Billy you don't know
what you are talking about

Love Paul

James Baker Hall

9.28.67/NYC

Dear Bill

　　　I am sorry
about all this but
it was unavoidable
I took a job in Atlanta
Kathleen did not
want to move again
and certainly one could not
blame her but
I was ready to kill
my boss
　　　　Now
we're back in NYC & I'm back
at Thompson　They fired
the little piece of shit
If I believed in triumphs
I would take this to be one

　　　　　I have never
been more or less than I am
irritable selfish pained
at what I see and cannot
see in time　I speak
more often than not
in a passion
We all know that

The doctor assures us
the dolefulness is nothing
to get upset about

But do you know that I see
you
every morning
at my breakfast
you
put your finger
in my coffee
& eat my cigarettes
you
untie my shoes
you
come out
of the door
as I go in
I shout at you
& receive for answer
the ultimate look eyes
quiet not scornful
He is so much like
you
& the thing is
like you
quiet gentle complex
enigmatic
It is enough to drive me
insane
But since I am insane
already & accept
the extranatural
then okay okay
I should adopt him
I should have adopted him
years ago but
still I cannot

James Baker Hall

I try to be good
to him
worrisome & protective
but we are all strange
to one another still
still

Things are difficult
to keep end to end
I do what I can
we all do what we can
& it is not good enough
by many times over

I do not think practically
I should adopt him
until we settle down
to one another/

The new child
is a new child
what more can one say

I will come to love her
I am sure as I have the first
but all I can see now
is that she has nothing
between her legs
nothing

Love Paul

* * *

Listen the boy is fine please
don't worry   He wants to be
a ballplayer like you
                    I must go
& barbecue can you believe it
I am sure you can

James Baker Hall

4.14.69 / Mt. Kisco

Dear Bill

             Kathleen called you
before we had a chance to talk
about it
         If the young man
needs a private school
I will see to it
that he goes
to a private school
Under no circumstances
are you to send money
You have your own family
and you are an artist
Money is not a problem
It is too early to tell
exactly what the trouble is
He does not know himself
why he behaves this way

Certainly he is bright
and should have no trouble
with class work/

My quarrel with poets
like Ciardi is their use
of naughty words   The trouble
with civilized people is
they have no understanding
of manners
or of anything else

Perhaps I should cut
myself
& sew
the issue up
in my mouth what
do you think

       Ciardi
with his shocking birdturds
is among the twenty million
on the other side of the TV
& I sell him too whatever
I choose   I am more cunning
than Odysseus   I sell him
Michelins for his TR-4
& he thinks because he knows
what is happening it makes
a difference but
it does not
       I think
of the millions sitting there
in the blue light night
after night the sweet
flypaper of their empty eyes
their empty lives
hanging there
in the blue light
waiting to be had
& I choose my images
with care

Yr fateful servant

Praeder

James Baker Hall

* * *

                Listen
about your novel I am
glad you brought it up
but let's drop it okay
It was your story too
& still is & still is
& anyway it was a long time ago
& in another country
& anyway the wench
is dead
                Who you
sent copies to
is your business

I won't say
I did not hate
you at the time
because I did

Don't forget who taught you
what poetry is Billy

Love Paul

Michael Hall

James Baker Hall

is the current Poet Laureate of Kentucky. *Praeder's Letters* is his sixth book of poems. *The New Yorker, The Paris Review, Poetry, The American Poetry Review,* and *The Kenyon Review* are among the many magazines to have published his work. He has received an NEA fellowship in poetry writing and has won both Pushcart and O. Henry prizes. He lives with his wife, fiction writer Mary Ann Taylor-Hall, in the Kentucky countryside, and teaches at the University of Kentucky.